HUNTING: PURSUING WILD GAME!™

ON THE WALL

RECORD-BREAKING HARVESTS

CHRISTINE POOLOS

rosen publishing's rosen central

New York

Published in 2013 by The Rosen Publishing Group, Inc.
29 East 21st Street, New York, NY 10010

First Edition

Library of Congress Cataloging-in-Publication Data

Poolos, Christine.
On the wall: record-breaking harvests/Christine Poolos.—1st ed.
p. cm.—(Hunting: pursuing wild game!)
Includes bibliographical references and index.
ISBN 978-1-4488-8277-9 (library binding)—ISBN 978-1-4488-8288-5 (pbk.)—
ISBN 978-1-4488-8289-2 (6-pack)
1. Big game hunting—North America. 2. Hunting trophies—North America. I. Title.
SK40.P66 2013
799.2'6—dc23

2012026584

Manufactured in the United States of America

CPSIA Compliance Information: Batch #W13YA: For further information, contact Rosen Publishing, New York, New York, at 1-800-237-9932.

CONTENTS

INTRODUCTION

Humans have been hunting for thousands of years, probably since before the Stone Age (approximately 4500–2000 BCE). In North America, Native Americans used weapons such as spears and bows and arrows to kill their game, which provided them with meat, hides, and bones with which to make tools. When the first Europeans began to colonize the eastern shores of America, they fished and hunted for sustenance to supplement their crops. As pioneers moved westward, hunting was used as a source of currency by trappers, who traded and sold valuable pelts. Hunting for sport was reserved for the wealthy, who had leisure time to embark on such expeditions.

In the United States today, hunting and harvesting is a popular recreation undertaken by those who like to spend time outdoors connecting with nature. Many are energized by the challenge of tracking a buck through the woods, landing it, and feasting on the year's supply of venison in their freezer. According to the U.S. Fish and Wildlife Service, an estimated 12.5 million people embark on hunting trips in the United States per year. About 10.7 million of those are big game pursuers, those who look for deer, elk, caribou, and other large animals.

Game is any animal that is hunted for food or for sport. Animals such as pheasant, turkeys, foxes,

More than ten million people in the United States embark on big game hunting expeditions each year. Many are pursuing deer, like this red deer stag.

squirrels, ducks, rabbits, and other small creatures are considered small game. Big game are larger animals that are targets of hunters, such as deer, moose, and elk. We also may think of exotic species that would be found on a safari, such as giraffes, elephants, and tigers, although they are not hunted in North America.

In the United States, sportspeople must go through certain steps before they can hunt big game. First, they must check their local state's laws and regulations. This information can be found on the Web site of the state's department of natural resources. Each type of game has its own season, and licenses and tags must be obtained within that season. Also, it is necessary for all hunters using firearms to have the proper permits for their weapons. Each state has limits as to how many animals a hunter may harvest. There are even rules about how much of the color orange must be worn in the field.

CHAPTER 1

Big Game Trophies

Many people who hunt big game are seeking a trophy, that is, a souvenir from the animal they have harvested. Picture a den with an elk's head and horns mounted to the wall, or a stuffed cougar ready to pounce in a natural history museum. Some hunters seek trophies as reminders of their expeditions, but others aim to make the record books.

There are two major organizations in North America that keep records of the largest big game trophies harvested. The Boone and Crockett Club is the best known and most widely regarded. According to its Web site, Boone and Crocket accepts "all legally hunter-taken trophies and found trophies [that is, dead animals found by hunters], which means they can be taken with a rifle, bow, muzzle loader, handgun, crossbow, and shotgun." The Pope and Young Club is similarly respected. This club, however, accepts for consideration in its record books only trophies that are harvested using bow and arrow. These organizations have strict rules regarding measurements of the trophies, depending on the species.

Many hunters like to keep trophies of their harvests. This deer head has been preserved and mounted to hang on a wall.

Boone and Crockett

The Boone and Crockett Club was established in 1887 with the assistance of one of the United States' great conservationists, President Theodore Roosevelt. Named after frontiersmen Daniel Boone and Davey Crockett, the club was founded to enforce regulations on hunting. At that time, rampant and unrestricted hunting threatened the extinction of much of America's wildlife.

The Boone and Crockett Club framed a constitution that focused on the ethics of hunting. That constitution later was used as a foundation for the creation of hunting laws in states throughout the country. The club also instituted a scoring system that has been used for more than fifty years. Boone and Crockett publishes a book of its record trophies every six years.

The Boone and Crockett Club is the gold standard for the record keeping of harvested trophies. This is the record-holding Chadwick Ram, which is displayed in Boone and Crockett's headquarters in Missoula, Montana.

Pope and Young

The Pope and Young Club was founded in 1961 to honor trophy animals harvested by archers. The club owes a lot to Boone and Crockett, having based its tenets on that club's constitution. Named for Dr. Saxton Pope and Arthur Young, early-twentieth-century pioneer bow hunters, the club's formation was intended to draw attention to bow hunting, which had fallen in popularity.

According to its Web site, the club "conducts ongoing recording periods and every two years presents appropriate recognition to the finest specimens submitted. These biennial presentations honor the quality of

Theodore Roosevelt

Teddy Roosevelt is best known as the twenty-sixth president of the United States. He used his influence to address one of his pet causes: the country's diminishing natural resources. Roosevelt had visited the Badlands of North Dakota to hunt bison but was astonished to see how few were left, thanks to overhunting. In addition, he saw that the ecology of the area could no longer support wildlife there.

During his presidency, among many other achievements, Roosevelt created the U.S. Forest Service. He helped found the Boone and Crockett Club, which is committed to wildlife preservation, hunting regulations, and the recording of species. Perhaps most significant, he placed 230,000,000 acres (930,777 sq kilometers) of national parks, national forests, and wildlife preserves under protection.

individual examples of North American big game species and promote the ideals of fair chase."

General Requirements for Record Trophies

Both Boone and Crockett and Pope and Young have an extensive list of requirements, available on their Web sites, for trophy eligibility. Although Boone and Crockett's policy may be more inclusive with regard to how an animal is harvested, its policies are similar to Pope and Young's when it comes to record keeping.

Both clubs are strict about the tagging, processing, and registering of harvests. In addition, hunters must field dress and thoroughly clean their harvests, and then wait out the appropriate drying period before measurement.

Measuring

Once the appropriate drying period has elapsed and the hunter has cleaned the skull plate of his or her harvest, an official is called to measure the trophy. Both clubs have volunteer measurers who donate their time scoring the harvests for entry into the club's records. Officials score based on the measurements of antlers, horns, or skull, depending on the species. Mass and symmetry are taken into consideration, as well.

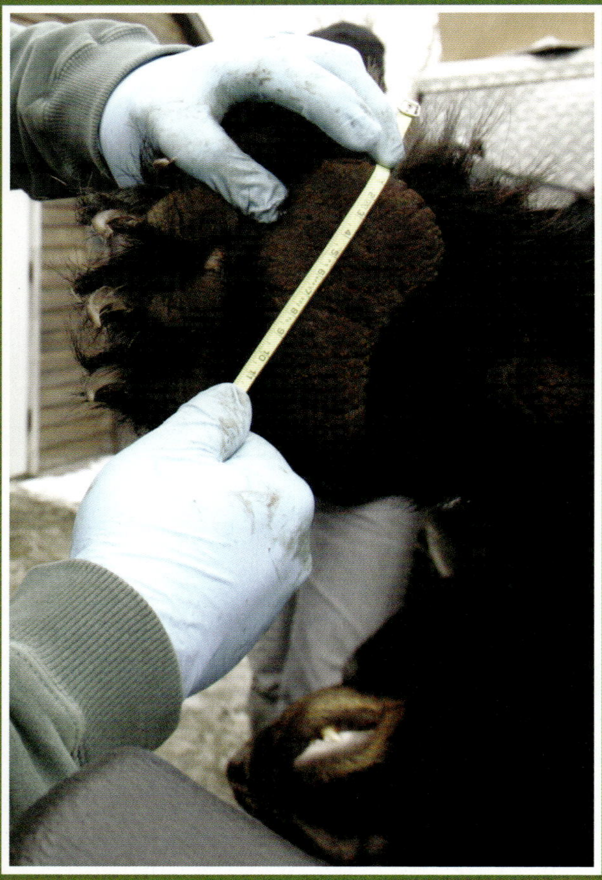

For a harvest to be eligible for record consideration, it must be measured by an official measurer. In the photo above, a bear paw is measured for size.

If the trophy meets the club's entry requirements, the hunter must fill out the appropriate paperwork and wait for the score to be considered official. Boone and Crockett features scoring worksheets for each animal on its Web site.

CHAPTER 2

Record Deer Harvests

Deer may be the most frequently harvested of all big game. Boone and Crockett and Pope and Young both keep records for trophies of ten species of deer, including typical and nontypical categories. Nontypical refers simply to the deer's antlers. While a typical rack exhibits symmetry and appears the way you would imagine perfect antlers to, a nontypical rack might have unmatched points. Nontypicals may have drop tines and other irregularities that negatively affect an ultimate score.

Scoring Deer Trophies

Deer trophies are scored using a series of measurements taken to the nearest one-eighth of an inch (0.3 centimeter). First, the number of points is recorded. Then, measurements are taken for the tip-to-tip

Deer are scored on the merits of their antlers. Taken into consideration are the span of the rack, the number of points, and individual measurements of the points.

spread, greatest spread, inside spread, length of normal and abnormal points, length of main beam, and circumferences.

Whitetail Deer

The record whitetail deer, according to Boone and Crockett, was shot by Milo N. Hanson in 1993 in Saskatchewan, Canada. Hanson found the deer not far from his farm. One of Hanson's neighbors had spotted a huge buck feeding in an alfalfa field, and Hanson and his fellow hunters reported sightings of the buck around the area throughout the summer. When deer hunting season began that fall, they formulated a plan to harvest the whitetail.

Just after a freshly fallen snow in November, someone sighted the buck entering a field. Hanson and his friends surrounded the field while one of them followed the deer's tracks. Suddenly, the buck came out, running just past Hanson, who fired shots but missed. After a chase, Hanson was able to get the buck in his crosshairs. Hanson said that harvesting that buck left him shaking.

A Boone and Crockett measurer scored the whitetail's rack at 214 4/8 inches (545 cm). It was a new record. The final, official score after the sixty-day drying period was 213 5/8 (542 cm). Hanson became a celebrity, as television crews, antler collectors, and magazine writers descended on his farm.

Pope and Young's record whitetail was taken out by Mel Johnson in 1965 in Peoria County, Illinois. That buck was scored at 204 4/8 inches (519 cm) and still reigns as the record whitetail to be harvested by bow and arrow. Johnson was bow hunting just twenty minutes from downtown Peoria when he spotted the buck and shot a couple of arrows, which punctured the buck's lungs. Although the whitetail bounded away, Johnson found it lying in a field not far away.

Boone and Crockett's record for a nontypical whitetail deer is one that died of natural causes and was picked up by the Missouri Department of Conservation just 20 miles (32 km) from downtown St. Louis in 1981. The deer scored 337 7/8 (858 cm) and weighed 250 pounds (113 kilograms). An outside spread of 33 3/8 inches (84 cm) was impressive, especially for a suburban deer.

Pope and Young's record is held by Michael Beatty, of Greene County, Ohio, who set off some scent bombs on the edge of a cornfield and waited up in his tree stand, 18 feet (5.5 meters) off the ground. About an hour later, he sounded a call. Suddenly, an eight-pointer that Beatty had been tracking all summer emerged, but he couldn't get a clear shot, and the buck wandered off. Disappointed, Beatty tried a few more calls and rattled some antlers. To his surprise, another

Harvesting a deer such as this whitetail takes luck, skill, and, above all, patience. Sometimes, hunters must track a deer for hours or even days before the right opportunity arises.

buck emerged—this one much larger than the last. He had a clear shot and fired an arrow, and the buck ran off.

Beatty tracked the blood more than 250 yards (229 m) from where he'd shot at the buck. With darkness descending, Beatty decided to go home and return the next morning to find the buck. When he did, he realized it had dropped only 30 yards (27 m) from his tree stand. In January 2001, Boone and Crockett scored the 39-point rack at 304 6/8 (774 cm).

Coues Whitetail Deer

The Coues whitetail is a smaller deer found in just a few southwestern states.

Boone and Crockett's record typical Coues deer was harvested by Ed Stockwell in Arizona in 1953. After a fruitless day of hunting, Stockwell headed over a mountain on his way back to camp when he came upon a buck. The animal darted away, and Stockwell waited, then moved slowly in the direction the deer had taken. After a while, the buck emerged from behind a tree, and Stockwell fired his .300 Savage. Measuring 144 1/8 (366 cm), the buck was so massive that at first Stockwell thought it might be a regular whitetail, but it was confirmed as a Coues and was entered into the record books.

Pope and Young's record-holding typical Coues is a buck taken in 2001 in Arizona. Fireman Sergio Orozco showed extreme patience when he bagged a Coues officially scoring 130 1/8 (330 cm). Orozco first saw the huge buck on a day of bow hunting in August 2000, but the animal disappeared before he could do anything. Over the next few weeks, he returned to the area to look for the buck but came up empty. Archery season ended, and rifle season began, and Orozco worried that the buck would be harvested by a rifleman. As luck would have it, when archery season started up again in December, Orozco spotted the Coues.

Orozco spent two weeks stalking the buck. Still nothing. Finally, in January, the fireman glassed it: It was racing around with several doe. Orozco spent hours stalking and glassing up the mountain until finally he had his shot. He released two arrows that hit the buck, who bounded away. Orozco trailed the blood and finally found the animal in a heap under a tree. Orozco then called a friend to help him do a preliminary measure of the trophy. The Coues surpassed the previous record by a whopping ten points.

The record-holding nontypical Coues whitetail was taken by an unknown Native American hunter in 1971. The animal received a Boone and Crockett score of 196 2/8 (498 cm). The trophy's antlers were eleven points on the right and fifteen points on the left. Pope and Young's record is held by Nathan Lacost, who bagged a nontypical Coues in Arizona in 2008 with an official score of 127 1/8 (323 cm).

Mule Deer

Mule deer live in the western United States. Their antlers typically are not as large as those of their whitetail cousins. In 1972, Doug Burris Jr. went on a hunting trip with some friends. After most of the men bagged five-point bucks, Burris decided to pursue a larger deer that one of his friends had seen earlier. He first saw the buck along with two others about 500 yards (457 m) away. He knew this buck was special because he could make out its large rack without the aid of binoculars. He spent the next hour stalking the buck, when suddenly he nearly stepped on a bedded doe. In the commotion, the bucks Burris was stalking scattered, and Burris fired his .264 Winchester Magnum. Luck was on his side: Despite the unfocused shot, the largest buck collapsed. Boone and Crockett confirmed Burris's record with a final score of 226 4/8 (575 cm).

The record nontypical mule deer was harvested by Ed Broder in Alberta, Canada, way back in 1926. Broder was an accomplished gamesman who was tracking a moose in the snow when he noticed some fresh deer tracks. After several hours of tracking the deer, he finally had a clear shot and dropped the deer by firing his Winchester .32 Special. It was then that he realized what a tremendous buck he had harvested. The trophy hung mounted on his wall for thirty-six years before Boone and Crockett measured it and declared it a winner. The mule deer had forty-three scorable points and was officially scored at 355 2/8 (902 cm).

Mule deer are smaller than whitetail. They live in the western United States. Also called blacktail deer, they are recognized by their mulelike ears.

The bow-hunting record score for a typical mule deer is 205 0/8 (521 cm). It was taken by George Harms in 2009 in Hermosillo, Mexico. Pope and Young's record for a nontypical mule deer was set in Colorado in 1987, when Kenneth W. Plank received a score of 274 7/8 (698 cm).

Sitka Blacktail Deer

The Sitka is a subspecies of the mule deer, typically found in Alaska and British Columbia. Boone and Crockett's record score for the Sitka blacktail is 133 (338 cm), bagged by Peter Bond in 1970 in British Columbia.

Lester Miller's Story

Longtime hunter Lester Miller wrote about bagging his record-winning Columbia blacktail in Northwest Big Game, Inc.'s *Blacktail Legends of the Pacific Northwest*:

> *No animal has ever had the impact on me that this huge buck had when I looked down on him as he lay there on the side of that ridge. The antlers were awesome to see with their spread and color and symmetry…I placed the Game Department seal on a horn and field-dressed him, putting the liver and heart in my liver bag. With my hatchet, I cut alder poles, turning the carcass belly-down on them to cool-out while protected from the rain. With one last look at my magnificent (to me) buck, I hurried downstream to try and get help to get him out to the road. By my reckoning, the road was about three miles [5 km] away. Although this hunt began years ago, certain things are as clear now in my mind as they were then: the first time I saw him; the times he outsmarted me; and, of course the day his luck ran out.*

Each side had five points. The nontypical Sitka record goes to William B. Steele Jr. for his score of 134 (340 cm). The right side had five points; the left side had six. His harvest took place in Alaska.

Charles Hakari earned the record for Sitka taken by bow and arrow. Pope and Young scored his trophy, which was harvested in Alaska in 1987, at 116 3/8 (295 cm).

Columbian Blacktail

Columbian blacktail extend from British Columbia to California's Monterey Bay. The Boone and Crockett record holder for a typical Columbian blacktail is Lester H. Miller, who downed a ten-point buck

Columbian blacktail deer are found on the west coast of lower Canada and the upper United States. This buck was photographed in California.

in Lewis County, Washington. Boone and Crockett scored the trophy at 182 2/8 (463 cm). The record has held since 1953. Miller stalked the buck over the course of three years before finally getting his shot. The record for a nontypical Columbian blacktail is held by Frank S. Foldi. In 1962, his trophy, taken in Polk County, Oregon, scored 208 1/8 (528 cm).

Pope and Young's record holders are B.G. Shurtleff (typical) and James Decker (nontypical). Decker bagged his buck in Jackson County, Oregon, in 1988 with a score of 194 4/8 (494 cm). Shurtleff's trophy scored 172 2/8 (437.5 cm) and has held since 1969. Shurtleff was able to down the buck with just one arrow shot from a 10-yard (9-m) distance.

CHAPTER

Moose, Elk, and Caribou

Moose, elk, and caribou are hunted widely in North America, although they are not as plentiful as the more common species of deer. Moose have suffered from overhunting. Other populations have dwindled due to disease. Many states allow hunting these animals by lottery only and keep a short hunting season.

Scoring Trophy Moose, Elk, and Caribou

Subspecies of all three animals are scored using the same general requirements. Most antlers are judged according to some or all of the following criteria: number of points, point length, palm length and width, circumferences, inside spread, greatest spread, and length of main beam.

Due to a dwindling population, moose season is often abbreviated and limited by lottery. This moose was harvested in Maine and weighed in at 724 pounds (328 kg).

Trophy Moose

Moose are the largest species in the deer family. They tend to stay in the colder climates of the northern parts of North America. Moose have the greatest amount of antler material of all members of the deer family. The largest racks come from Alaska, Yukon, and the Northwest Territories.

Alaska-Yukon Moose

The Alaska is the largest moose subspecies. It can be found in the forests of Alaska and the Yukon. The highest-scoring moose taken by firearm was harvested in Alaska by John A. Crouse in 1994. Crouse was eager to take any moose he saw when he and some hunting buddies flew into Alaska. He saw one right away, lying in its bed. When it stood, Crouse took it down with a .270. It took Crouse and his buddies two full days to field dress the moose and pack it to get back to camp. When it came time to return home, the pilot had to send for a bigger plane in order to fit the antlers! Crouse's moose was scored at 261 5/8 (664 cm). The greatest spread was 65 1/8 inches (165 cm), and the palm length was approximately 54 inches (137 cm) on each side.

The bow-hunting record is held by Real Langlois, a guide from Canada who harvested his trophy in 2008 in the Yukon. Langlois drew the bull

Moose are found in other parts of the world. In Europe, they are called elk, not to be confused with the different species that Americans call elk.

with calls and rattling of special paddles that he had made. Within five minutes of sighting the moose, he had taken it down with one arrow from only 8 feet (2.4 m) away. The bull weighed 1,560 pounds (708 kg)! Langlois's harvest scored 249 1/8 (632 cm).

Canada Moose

It should come as no surprise that the top Canada moose trophies were harvested in Canada. The Boone and Crockett record holder is Michael Laub, for a thirty-one-point bull he took down in British Columbia in 1980. Laub had never even seen a moose before firing at the bull—on

The bull moose pictured above is walking in the snow of Gaspesie National Park in Quebec, Canada. During mating season, bull moose challenge each other for females.

horseback from 350 yards (320 m) away. It took several more shots before Laub scored the trophy. The antler spread was 63 inches (160 cm), and the palm width was approximately 22 inches (56 cm). After the drying period, Laub's official score was 242 (615 cm).

The bow-hunting record is held by Charles Roy, who took down his bull in Quebec. Roy's winning score of 222 1/8 (564 cm) has held the record since 1988.

Shiras Moose

The smallest of all the moose subspecies, the Shiras moose is found in Wyoming, Idaho, Utah, Colorado, Washington, Oregon, and Montana. Boone and Crockett's record-holding Shiras is a thirty-pointer shot by John Oakley in Wyoming. The bull's greatest spread was 53 inches (135 cm), and the palm length was just over 38 inches (96. 5cm). Oakley was scored at 205 4/8 (522 cm). It was an impressive feat, especially considering that the record has held for more than a half-century. Richard Jones took the Pope and Young record in 1987 with a bull he took down in 1987, also in Wyoming.

Trophy Elk

Two of North America's six subspecies of elk have become extinct. Boone and Crockett recognizes four types of trophy elk: American (typical and nontypical), Roosevelt, and tule.

American Elk

The record-winning typical American elk trophy was taken by the rifle of Alonzo Winters in 1968 in the mountains of Arizona. Winters got the thirteen-pointer when he was horseback riding with a friend in 1968. The rack sat for years in Winters's basement until after he died, when it was sold to an antiques buyer, who had it measured by Boone and Crockett. The rack made the history books, with a score of 442 5/8 (1,123 cm).

The bow-hunting record for typical American elk is held by former NFL lineman Shawn Patterson, from 2005. With the help of a guide, he was able to spot a massive bull and track it, often on his hands and knees to avoid giving himself away in the rocky conditions. Patterson

A bowhunter crouches in the woods, ready to fire a shot at an elk he has been tracking.

shot an arrow, and the two men left the area for a time, to allow the bull to expire. Only when he returned to find the massive creature did he see just what a trophy he'd gained. Pope and Young officially scored his trophy at 412 1/8 (1,046 cm).

The record-holding nontypical American elk (killed by firearm) belongs to Denny Austad, who harvested a twenty-three-point bull in Utah in 2008. The rack was scored at 478 5/8 (1,215 cm). That's almost 500 inches (1,270 cm) of antler! With the help of a guide, Austad pursued the bull for nearly two weeks before getting a clean shot.

Pope and Young's record nontypical American elk was bow hunted by Nick Franklin in Arizona. Franklin was six days into his hunting trip before he finally sighted and tracked the bull, known in those parts as "Grandpa." "As soon as I shot him, the arrow went clean through him and hit rock behind him," Franklin said. "When that happened, he picked his head up and looked over at the rocks to see what happened. He stood there for about three or four seconds, and then started moving off." The bull dropped not long after. It was later officially scored at 442 0/8 (1,123 cm).

Roosevelt Elk

The Roosevelt elk is the largest North American elk species. Its primary habitats are the rain forests of the Pacific Northwest. In 2002, Jason Ballard harvested Boone and Crockett's current record-holding Roosevelt. The elk, which Ballard took down in Oregon, received a final score of 404 6/8 (1,028 cm). The seventeen-pointer had an inside spread of 40 6/8 inches (103.5 cm). The length of the left main beam alone was 57 5/8 inches (146 cm).

Pope and Young's record for a bow-hunted Roosevelt elk is held by Clifford Hayden. Hayden arrowed the bull in Oregon in 1991. Pope and Young scored it at 378 6/8 inches (962 cm).

Tule Elk

The tule elk lives in the California grasslands. Boone and Crockett's winning tule was picked up in Glenn County in 2005. The sixteen-pointer scored a 379 (963 cm), with an inside spread of 39 3/8 inches (100 cm) and a 51-inch (129.5 cm) left main beam.

In 1990, bow hunter Audrey Goodnight took down a bull in Solano County that Pope and Young scored at 312 5/8 (794 cm). Goodnight has the distinction of being Pope and Young's first record holder in the tule elk category.

Trophy Caribou

Also known as reindeer, caribou can be found in the subarctic regions of North America. Many populations are in decline because of climate change. Boone and Crockett has defined the species for record-keeping purposes. Records are kept for five species of caribou.

Mountain Caribou

Mountain caribou live in the rain forest in the Pacific Northwest and British Columbia. The population of the mountain caribou is very low, and they are protected as an endangered species in the United States.

Paul Deuling harvested Boone and Crockett's record holder in 1988 in the Yukon's Pelly Mountains. The bull was a thirty-eight-pointer, with an inside spread of 40 inches (102 cm). Deuling was actually hunting sheep when he spotted an enormous caribou and realized he could use the meat. He fired on the elk from a distance of 10 yards (9 m) and watched it run for a few minutes before collapsing. Incredibly, Deuling didn't contact Boone and Crockett right away. The rack hung on his wall for years. When Deuling finally had his antlers measured, they were scored at 459 3/8 (1,167 cm) and went straight into Boone and Crockett's record book.

In 2004, Idaho bow hunter Pete Cintorino hired an outfitting guide to take him on a moose hunt in the Yukon. One day after bagging a huge moose, Cintorino spotted a herd of caribou, including its leader. He tracked the caribou a quarter-mile and got a clean shot from a 40-yard (37-m) distance. An elated Cintorino field dressed the animal, then packed up the meat and antlers and took them home. After the sixty-day drying period, Pope and Young scored the trophy at 416 4/8, a new world record.

Pete Cintorino's Caribou Harvest

Pope and Young record holder Pete Cintorino told *Bowhunter* magazine about the moment he scored his trophy.

> *As I closed the gap, my heart and mind raced a hundred miles an hour. Watch the wind, wait for a good shot, keep your head down! I kept thinking. Finally within striking distance, I pulled out my rangefinder. My hand was shaking so badly I couldn't hold it steady but finally got a reading—58 yards (53 m). At home on the practice range, I shoot fairly well at that distance, but on an animal, that was too far. So I forced myself to sneak closer, crawling on all fours through the wet moss and low willows to gain 20 more yards (18 m)...Just as I was getting ready to draw my bow, the bull started to move off. Instantly, my natural reflexes took over. Kneeling on a grass tussock to gain elevation, I centered the sight pin on his chest, and when he stopped one last time to look back, my arrow flew true, a perfect heart shot. The caribou traveled less than 40 yards (37 m) before collapsing in the tundra.*

Woodland Caribou

Woodland caribou are considered endangered in the United States. Where they once could be found in the forests of the North, from Maine to Washington, they are now down to one herd that roams Idaho, Washington, and British Columbia.

Woodland caribou bulls forage in the Tonquin Valley of Canada's Jasper National Park in Alberta.

Reflecting the subspecies status, both records are quite old. Boone and Crockett's record is from a 1910 woodland caribou that was owned by H. Casmir de Rham. It scored 419 5/8 (1,065.5 cm), with thirty-seven points and an inside spread of 43 2/8 inches (110 cm). Pope and Young's record is held by Dempsey Cape, who arrowed the caribou in 1966 in Newfoundland. That caribou scored 345 2/8 (877 cm).

Barren Ground Caribou

This subspecies is found primarily in the Northwest Territories. Daniel Dobbs holds Boone and Crockett's record for a caribou he harvested in Alaska in 1999. The forty-two-pointer scored 477 (1,212 cm). The inside spread of the rack was 38 3/8 inches (97 cm). Pope and Young's record is held by Dennis Burdick, whose trophy scored 448 6/8 (1,140 cm) in 1984.

Central Canada Barren Ground Caribou

This subspecies is smaller and can be found in Nunavut, Canada. Boone and Crockett recognizes a fifty-five-point caribou harvested by Donald Hotter in 1994 in the Northwest Territories. The length of each main beam was approximately 49 inches (124 cm) and the inside spread was 40 3/8 (102 cm). Boone and Crockett scored the trophy at 433 3/8 (1,101 cm).

In the same area, in the same year, Pope and Young's record winner was taken down by bow hunter Al Kuntz. Kuntz traveled from Minnesota to enlist the services of a guide at Humpy Lake. While observing a herd of caribou, Kuntz turned around to see a bull. The bull pegged Kuntz and his guide and took off. The two men traveled by boat to find it. Tempted to use a rifle, Kuntz waited it out until he was able to come within 40 yards (37 m) of the bull. At last, he drew his bow and released the arrow, which hit the caribou's chest and brought it down instantly.

Pope and Young officially scored the trophy at 420 6/8 (1,069 cm). It was a full 35 inches (89 cm) larger than the previous record holder. Just as Kuntz was heading back home, he ran into Don Hotter, who would harvest his Boone and Crockett trophy just one week later!

Quebec-Labrador Caribou

The habitat of this subspecies is the tundra, and, true to its name, it can be found in Quebec and Labrador, Canada. Boone and Crockett's record dates back to 1931, to a caribou harvested by Zack Elbow in Labrador. The official score was 474 6/8 (1,206 cm) on the fifty-two-pointer, which had an inside spread of 58 2/8 inches (148 cm). Elbow hunted the caribou for meat, not for sport.

Pope and Young's record-winning caribou was arrowed by Carol Ann Mauch in 1984 in Quebec. This animal was quite a bit smaller, scoring 430 0/8 (1,092 cm).

CHAPTER 4

SHEEP AND HORNED GAME

Serious hunters are drawn to the challenge of pursuing sheep and horned game. Some of these animals are protected. Sheep are scored according to measurements of greatest spread, tip-to-tip spread, length of horn, circumference of horn, and circumference of base. Horned game are scored on measurements of tip-to-tip spread, inside spread of main beams, length of horn, circumference of base, horn circumference, and length of prongs.

Trophy Sheep

Trophy sheep are among the most protected of all hunted game in the United States. The nineteenth century saw a surge in their harvest, mostly because of the animal's desirable meat. The consequence was a dwindling population. Today,

thanks to conservation efforts and continuing underdevelopment of their habitat, sheep are enjoying invigorated status.

Bighorn Sheep

The horns that give bighorn their name can weigh up to 30 pounds (14 kg). The animals themselves can reach 300 pounds (136 kg). Bighorns

Bighorn rams fight in Wyoming. Both Boone and Crockett's and Pope and Young's record-winning bighorns were harvested in Alberta, Canada.

range in the cooler mountain regions of the United States and Canada, including the Rocky Mountains.

Guinn Crousen took down Boone and Crockett's biggest bighorn in 2000. Harvested in Alberta, Canada, the sheep scored 208 3/8 (529 cm). Its tip-to-tip spread was 23 1/8 inches (58 cm); its horns were approximately 47 inches (119 cm) long and 15 inches (38 cm) around at their greatest point.

Pope and Young's record holder is Todd Kirk. Kirk speared a sheep in Alberta in 1998 that scored 199 5/8 (507 cm).

Boy Scouts Save the Bighorns

In 1936, Major Frederick Burnham noticed that the population of desert bighorn in Arizona was headed toward extinction because of hunting and destruction of their habitat. He called on George Miller, head of the Boy Scout Council, which was headquartered in Phoenix.

Miller enlisted the help of the Arizona Boy Scouts in launching a campaign to preserve the animal. Scouts across the state participated in a "save the bighorn" poster contest, wore the bighorn logo on their uniforms, and promoted their cause on the radio and in school assemblies across the state.

Thanks to a groundswell of support for the scouts, on January 18, 1939, President Roosevelt signed an executive order to set aside 1.5 million acres (6,070 sq km) to form the Kofa National Wildlife Refuge and the Cabeza Prietas National Wildlife Refuge. The refuges have succeeded in increasing the number of sheep, and credit goes to the efforts of the Boy Scouts. The bighorn is the official mascot of the Arizona Boy Scouts.

Desert Sheep

These sheep live in the desert regions of the southwestern United States and Mexico.

The largest desert sheep to be harvested using a firearm was taken by a Native American in Mexico in 1940. The horns were 43 inches (109 cm) long, and the tip-to-tip spread was 25 5/8 inches (65 cm). Boone and Crockett scored it at 205 1/8 (521 cm).

The record-holding desert sheep taken by bow and arrow was harvested by Jim Hens in 2007 in New Mexico. That sheep scored 178 6/8 (454 cm). Hens attracted some controversy for paying $300,000 for his tag.

Dall sheep stand atop a mountain peak. The species can be found in Alaska, the Yukon territory, and the Northwest Territories.

Dall Sheep

Dall sheep live in the subarctic mountains of Alaska, the Northwest Territories, and the Yukon. Harry Swank harvested Boone and Crockett's winner in 1961 in the mountains of Alaska. It scored 189 6/8 (482 cm) overall. The sheep's spread was 34 3/8 inches (87 cm), and its horns were approximately 48 inches (122 cm) long and 14 inches (35.5 cm) in circumference at their largest point.

The Pope and Young record is 171 0/8 (434 cm), for a Dall taken by Tony Russ in 1988 in Alaska.

Stone Sheep

Native to the American Northwest, the Stone sheep is a subspecies of the Dall.

In the wilds of British Columbia, hunter Lee Sherman Chadwick harvested a Stone that was scored 196 6/8 (500 cm) by Boone and Crockett. The spread was 31 inches (79 cm), and each horn was just over 50 inches (127 cm). The Chadwick ram, as it is known, has been the record holder since it was harvested in 1936. Because of land development in British Columbia, experts say the record will likely remain untested.

Stanley Walchuk took Pope and Young's winning Stone sheep in 1992 in British Columbia, with a score of 174 2/8 (442.5 cm).

Horned Game

Boone and Crockett and Pope and Young include several animals in the category of horned game. Records are kept for pronghorn, Rocky Mountain goat, bison, and musk ox trophies.

Pronghorn

Once plentiful in North America, pronghorn were near extinction by the early twentieth century. Thanks to conservation efforts, the population is somewhat bolstered today. Two pronghorn subspecies are considered endangered.

Boone and Crockett recognizes both David Meyer and Dylan Woods as record holders, each with a score of 95 (241 cm). Woods harvested his antelope first, in 2000. The college student was hunting without having scouted much in preparation when he stumbled upon a big buck and fired his weapon. The first shot missed, so he tried again. The horns measured 19 inches (48 cm) on one side and 17 (43 cm) on the other. Inside spread was 11 7/8 (30 cm).

Meyer filmed his buck in Arizona at the start of the summer of 2002 and reviewed the tape for two months before setting out to find it. Stalking it was a challenge because the landscape didn't allow any coverage. Meyer crawled and stalked for twelve hours before getting his shot, which he missed, much like Woods. Days later, he had another chance, which was a success. He had seen the pronghorn on tape and through his high-powered optics and knew it was a trophy worth taking, but he was even more impressed upon closer inspection. The horns measured just over 17 inches (43 cm) and had an inside spread of 10 1/8 (25.5 cm).

Marvin Zieser holds the bow-hunting pronghorn record. In 1995, he arrowed an antelope in Arizona that scored 91 4/8 (232 cm). During the summer of 1995, Zieser shot video footage of an unusually tall buck and set his sights on it once the season began. However, once in the field, he was faced with a common hunter's quandary. A slightly less-impressive pronghorn repeatedly surfaced while Zieser scouted his buck. Zieser was reluctant to take a shot at this animal because he wanted to use his permit on the big one. Eventually, he realized he couldn't pass up the opportunity: he took down the smaller buck. It was only when he approached the animal that he realized how large it actually was—large enough to earn him the top pronghorn award in Pope and Young's record books.

Rocky Mountain Goat

Rocky Mountain goats live in the cool elevations of the Rocky Mountains and the Cascade Mountain Range. Their superior climbing skills make them a challenge for hunters to stalk. Two Rocky Mountain goats hold the record from Boone and Crockett, with scores of 56 6/8 (144 cm). The first, taken by E. C. Haase in 1949 in British Columbia, had a horn spread of 9 2/8 inches (23.5 cm). Each horn was 12 inches (30.5 cm) long, with base circumferences of 6 4/8 (16. 5 cm). Fifty years later, also in British Columbia, Gernot Wober harvested a goat with a spread of 8 7/8 inches (23 cm). The horns were 11 7/8 inches (30 cm) and 10 6/8 inches (27 cm), with circumferences of 6 4/8 (16.5 cm).

In 2006, bow hunter Shad Wheeler took down the record-holding goat in British Columbia. Wheeler's trophy did not come easily. He and his guide spotted

A hunter shows off his trophy, taken in a Rocky Mountain goat hunt.

the goat on the first day of their expedition but had trouble getting close to it because of the icy conditions of the mountains where the goats herded. On the ninth day, Wheeler finally got within 25 yards (23 m) of the animal, took a shot, and missed. Fortunately for the hunter, the goat was distracted by a wolf's howls and by falling rocks and ice. Wheeler's second arrow hit its target, but it wasn't smooth sailing from there. The goat fell down a cliff more than 75 feet (23 m). Wheeler and his guide had to rappel down the icy slopes to retrieve his trophy, which Pope and Young scored at 53 0/8 (135 cm).

Although closely related to the sheep, musk ox can reach weights of 900 pounds (408 kg).

Musk Ox

The musk ox is an arctic animal closely related to sheep and goats. It weighs an average of 600 pounds (272 kg) but can reach 900 pounds (408 kg). In North America, musk ox are found in the arctic regions of Canada and the United States.

There are two Boone and Crockett record holders. Musk ox harvested by Craig Scott in 2002 and by Jim Shockey in 2006 both scored 129 (328 cm). Scott's was taken in the Northwest Territories. The tip-to-tip spread was 27 1/8 inches (69 cm); the horns were 29 5/8 (75 cm) and 28 3/8 inches (71 cm) long, with a circumference of 6 2/8 (16 cm) and 5 4/8 (14 cm). Shockey got his in Nunavut, Canada. The tip-to-tip spread was 30 4/8 (77.5 cm), and each horn was just over 28 inches (71 cm) long, with circumferences of 5 7/8 (15 cm) and 6 3/8 (16 cm).

There is also a tie for the Pope and Young top honor. Bob Black and William Cox both scored 127 2/8 (323 cm) for their trophies. Black arrowed his in the Northwest Territories in 1996, and Cox took his in the same area in 1998.

CHAPTER 5

Bears and Cats

Boone and Crockett and Pope and Young recognize more exotic big game, as well. Select species of bears and game cats are eligible for record consideration.

Trophy Bears

Four subspecies of bear are eligible. Calipers are used to measure a bear's skull to the nearest one-sixteenth of an inch. Measurements are taken for the greatest length of the skull (without the lower jaw) and the greatest width.

Black Bear

The black bear is the most common bear in North America. It is also the smallest. Boone and Crockett's record black bear was an animal that was picked up in Utah in 1975. The

An official checks the tag on a bear harvested during a bear hunt in Maryland. Animals must be harvested legally to be eligible for records.

skull measured 14 12/16 inches (37.5 cm) long and 8 14/16 inches (23 cm) wide. The final score was 23 10/16 (60 cm). The record for a bow-hunted black bear is not far off: 23 3/16 (59 cm). That bear was arrowed by Robert Shuttleworth in California in 1993.

Grizzly Bear

The grizzly is a type of brown bear that lives in the western region of North America. Boone and Crockett's record grizzly scored 27 13/16 (71 cm).

It was picked up in Alaska in 1976. The skull's greatest length was 17 4/16 (44 cm), with a width of 10 9/16 (27 cm).

Pope and Young's record is held by Dennis Dunn. Dunn took his grizzly in Alaska in 2004. The skull's official score was 26 3/16 (67 cm).

A hunter poses with his grizzly bear catch in Alaska. It is recommended that hunters bring cameras on their expeditions to record their harvests.

Alaska Brown Bear

The Alaska brown bear can weigh more than 3,000 pounds (1,361 kg), thanks to a steady diet of salmon. Roy Lindsley harvested Boone and Crockett's record holder in 1952 on Kodiak Island, Alaska. The official score was 30 12/16 (78 cm). The skull's length was 17 15/16 inches (46 cm), with a width of 12 13/16 inches (33 cm). Bow hunter Jack Brittingham holds Pope and Young's record with a score of 29 3/16 (74 cm). There is amazing video of this 2004 harvest online.

Polar Bear

Polar bears live around the Arctic Circle. The United States considers the polar bear a threatened species and thus strictly limits trophies brought back to the country from Canadian expeditions. The bow-hunting

A polar bear hide is stretched and dried in the sun. Postharvest, trophies must be properly dressed and preserved.

record is held by Jimmie Ryan, who took his polar bear in the Northwest Territories in 2008. That bear scored 26 10/16 (67 cm).

Shelby Longoria traveled all the way from Mexico to Alaska to harvest his record-breaking polar bear in 1963. He fired on the bear on loose ice and nearly died trying to retrieve his trophy from the chilling water. The skull measured 18 8/16 inches (47 cm) long and 11 7/16 inches (29 cm) wide, earning it a Boone and Crockett score of 29 15/16 (76 cm).

What to Do Postharvest

Experienced hunters know that proper field dressing is the difference between having a museum-quality wall trophy and having only a story about the experience. First, make arrangements with a taxidermist before embarking on a hunting expedition. Second, along with weapons, optics, and other gear, hunters should pack a camera to document the harvest. Third, the hunter should bring a sharp knife with which to field dress the harvest. Finally, it is important to have clean bags in which to store the meat and, unless temperatures are cold, a cooler to preserve the meat.

Hunters must know the tagging and dressing laws of the state in which they are hunting. Failure to properly tag a harvest can result in confiscation. When field dressing, blood and other fluids must be wiped clean from the animal so that bacteria will not break down the fur or hair.

Finally, what good is a trophy if you can't get it home? Many hunters don't consider how they will retrieve their harvested animal. Oftentimes, they are miles from their truck or horse, and they must come back to get the carcass. It is a good idea to mark the carcass with something that will be visible upon return.

Trophy Cats

The cougar and the jaguar are the big game cats eligible for Boone and Crockett records. The cougar, also known as the puma or panther, is found in great numbers in many areas of North America. The jaguar can be found in the southern states, Mexico, and farther south. It is considered "near threatened" on the endangered scale, because

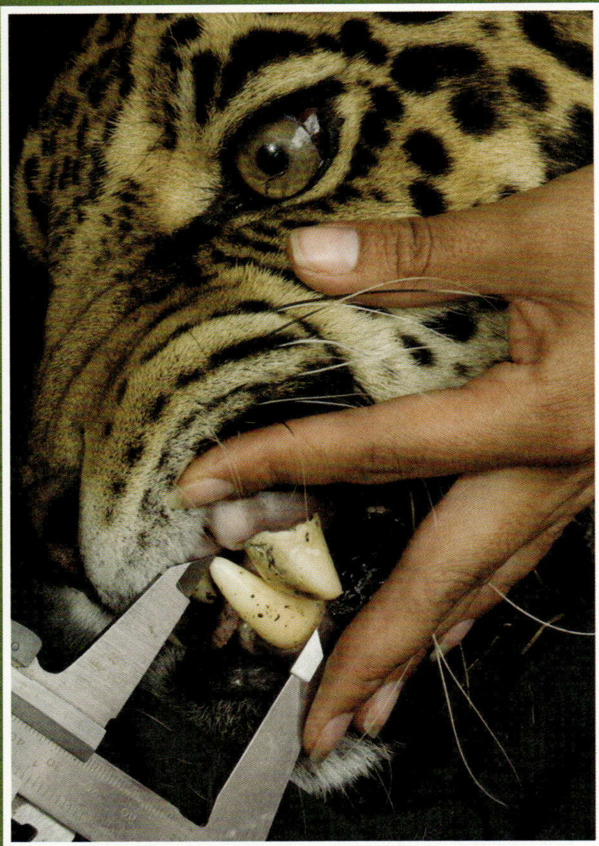

A jaguar's teeth are measured using a caliper. Eligible cat trophies are judged according to skull measurements.

of development of its habitat. Trophy cats are scored similarly to bears, adding the skull's length (without the lower jaw) and the skull's width.

Cougar

Douglas Schuk harvested Boone and Crockett's winning cougar in 1979 in British Columbia. The skull's length was 9 9/16 inches (24 cm) and its width was 6 11/16 (17 cm), earning Schuk a score of 16 4/16 (41 cm). Bow hunter Scott Moore's winning cat was arrowed in Wyoming in 1993, with an official score of 16 1/6 (40 cm).

Jaguar

C. J. McElroy took down the record jaguar back in 1965 in Mexico. The skull of the cat was 10 15/16 inches (28 cm) long and 7 8/16 inches wide (19 cm), making its final score 18 7/16 inches (47 cm). There is no Pope and Young record for jaguar.

CHAPTER 6

PRESERVATION AND CONSERVATION

It may seem counterintuitive, but most hunters will tell you that they have a deep respect and love for animals and nature. All of the top hunting organizations have strict statements regarding hunting ethics. Sportsmen and sportswomen like the challenge of hunting, but they also are interested in preserving our world's natural resources.

The harvesting of certain animals can help keep populations in check, which helps to keep a balanced ecosystem by maintaining populations of predators and natural resources. In addition, hunters pay quite a bit of money toward the conservation effort. The purchase of hunting licenses and taxes paid on hunting equipment go toward funding state game-management programs.

A game warden checks the license of a hunter who has harvested a deer. The purchase of mandatory licenses helps fund game-management programs.

North American Model of Wildlife Conservation

In 1842, in a case called *Martin v. Waddell*, the Supreme Court set the precedent that natural resources are free to all and are to be available to present and future generations. This ruling resulted in the Public Trust Doctrine. In no time, concerned hunters and conservationists in Canada joined their counterparts in the United States (including Theodore Roosevelt and the Boone and Crockett Club) to create the North American Model of Wildlife Conservation.

This model suggests that wildlife be managed through applied science and recreational hunting. The model is based on two fundamental

Conservation Education

Many hunting organizations such as Boone and Crockett, state game departments, and even zoos offer education about hunting and conservation to school-aged kids. They believe that today's kids are not connected with the natural world and that immersing them in it will teach them about natural habitats and fragile and endangered ecosystems.

Boone and Crockett alone offers several education programs focusing on different aspects of ecology. In addition, the club hosts the Leopold Education Project, an interdisciplinary program that "teach[es] the public about humanity's ties to the natural world and...provide[s] leadership in the effort to conserve and protect the earth's natural resources."

beliefs: that the resources of America belong to all citizens of North America and that these resources should be sustained.

Ethics

Boone and Crockett helped set the standard for hunting ethics that are practiced in the United States today. In recognition of the importance of conservation in preserving game animal population, the club states on its Web site a list of tenets that should be followed by every hunter:

1. Obey all applicable laws and regulations.
2. Respect the customs of the locale where the hunting occurs.
3. Exercise a personal code of behavior that reflects favorably on your abilities and sensibilities as a hunter.

Part of the sport of hunting is the respect participants must have for the land and also for their prey. Each state has its own laws that hunters must observe.

4. Attain and maintain the skills necessary to make the kill as certain and quick as possible.
5. Behave in a way that will bring no dishonor to either the hunter, the hunted, or the environment.
6. Recognize that these tenets are intended to enhance the hunter's experience of the relationship between predator and prey, which is one of the most fundamental relationships of humans and their environment.

Fair Chase

Fair chase is the ethical, sportsmanlike, and lawful pursuit and taking of any free-ranging, wild, native North American big game animal in a manner that does not give the hunter an improper advantage over such animals. Most hunters strive to maintain a strong field ethic, even beyond the law. For instance, there are many situations that are not illegal, but they may be unethical, such as firing at an animal from a great distance. Although that is perfectly legal, there are several moral implications, such as the chance of wounding rather than killing the animal

Hunting is a sport that can be enjoyed by families. Here, a father gives his son tips.

cleanly. Hunters must have defined ideas of their purpose and consider their place in relation to the animal.

Preservation and Records Keeping

Countless Web sites exist that give hunters a platform to defend their sport and champion their conservation efforts. If hunting does indeed help preserve our natural resources, then what role, if any, does record

Hunting trophies are kept not just for posterity, but also to honor the animal. Taxidermists have the job of preserving trophies, as shown in the photo above.

keeping play in this very important pursuit? It is one thing to help maintain proper levels of an animal population or to harvest meat, but is it going too far to measure and record them? And to hang trophies on our walls?

The Web site HuntFairChase.com makes a case for the importance of record books such as those of Boone and Crockett and Pope and Young. Bragging rights aside, these records can be seen as history books for big game hunting. As well, they are valuable resources for game managers who track the success of their programs. Perhaps, too, they bring awareness to conservation efforts.

So the next time you see a deer head mounted on a wall or a stuffed grizzly at a natural history museum, think of the person who harvested it. And then remember the history behind it: all the conservationists, lawmakers, game managers, and hunters who worked to preserve our natural resources.

Glossary

big game Large animals that are pursued by hunters, such as deer, elk, moose, and bears.

caliper A pronglike instrument used to measure.

circumference The distance around something.

drop tine The abnormal growth of a rack's tine in a downward direction.

drying period A mandatory period during which an animal carcass is removed of moisture and shrinks slightly, before being measured.

fair chase The ethical and lawful pursuit and harvesting of big game animals in a manner that does not give the hunter an improper or unfair advantage.

field dress The postharvest stage of removing the animal's internal organs.

glass To view through high-powered optics.

greatest spread The measurement between perpendiculars at a right angle to the center line of the skull.

inside spread The measurement at a right angle to the center line of the skull between main beams.

points Scorable prongs or protrusions of antlers.

stalk To track, observe, and follow an animal being hunted.

symmetry When both halves of a rack are similar or exactly the same.

tag The process of affixing the legal tag to a harvested animal.

tip-to-tip spread The measurement between the tips of a rack's main beams.

trophy A souvenir from a harvested animal.

For More Information

Boone and Crockett Club
250 Station Drive
Missoula, MT 59801
(406) 542-1888
Web site: http://www.boone-crockett.org

The mission of the Boone and Crockett Club is to promote the conservation and management of wildlife, especially big game, and its habitat; to preserve and encourage hunting; and to maintain the highest ethical standards of fair chase and sportsmanship in North America. According to the club, you don't have to have a trophy in the record book to belong to the Boone and Crockett Club, just a passion for big game and the hunting of them.

Canadian Wildlife Federation
350 Michael Cowpland Drive
Kanata, ON K2M 2W1
Canada
(800) 563-9453
Web site: http://www.cwf-fcf.org/en

According to its Web site, the Canadian Wildlife Federation is a charitable organization that works with Canadians to make a difference to the kind of legacy left behind, not just for wildlife, but also for children.

Ontario Federation of Anglers and Hunters (OFAH)
4601 Guthrie Drive
P.O. Box 2800
Peterborough, ON K9J 8L5
Canada

(705) 748-6324
Web site: http://www.ofah.org
The Ontario Federation of Anglers and Hunters is Canada's oldest organization for wildlife and fish management. OFAH promotes the rights of hunters and anglers.

Pope and Young Club
273 Mill Creek Road
P.O. Box 548
Chatfield, MN 55923
(507) 867-4144
Web site: http://www.pope-young.org
The Pope and Young Club is dedicated to the concerns and achievements of bow hunters. The club is patterned after the Boone and Crockett Club.

Theodore Roosevelt Conservation Partnership
1660 L Street NW, Suite 208
Washington, DC, 20036
(202) 639-8727
Web site: http://www.trcp.org
The Theodore Roosevelt Conservation Partnership strengthens laws, policies, and practices affecting fish and wildlife conservation by leading partnerships that influence decision makers.

U.S. Fish and Wildlife Service
1849 C Street NW
Washington, DC 20240
(800) 344-9453

Web site: http://www.fws.gov

The mission of the U.S. Fish and Wildlife Service is working with others to conserve, protect, and enhance fish, wildlife, plants, and their habitats for the continuing benefit of the American people.

Wildlife Conservation Society
2300 Southern Boulevard
Bronx, New York 10460
(718) 220-5100
Web site: http://www.wcs.org

The Wildlife Conservation Society has the mission to save wildlife and wild places across the globe. The organization protects many of the world's iconic creatures in the United States and abroad.

Web Sites

Due to the changing nature of Internet links, Rosen Publishing has developed an online list of Web sites related to the subject of this book. This site is updated regularly. Please use this link to access this list:

http://www.rosenlinks.com/HUNT/Wall

For Further Reading

Boone and Crockett Club. *Records of North American Big Game*. Thirteenth Edition. Missoula, MT: Boone and Crockett Club, 2011.

Carpenter, Tom. *Big Game Hunting: Bear, Deer, Elk, Sheep, and More*. Minneapolis, MN: Lerner Books, 2013.

Cassell, Jay, ed. *The Best Hunting Stories Ever Told*. New York, NY: Skyhorse Publishing, 2010.

Hisey, Glenn, ed. *Bowhunting Big Game Records of North America*. Chatfield, MN: Pope and Young Club, 2005.

Lamade, Mike. *Breathtaking Bowhunts: A Collection of Bowhunting Adventures*. Eynon, PA: Tribute Books, 2006.

Lundgren, Julie K. *Hunting*. Vero Beach, FL: Rourke Publishing, 2010.

Peterson, Judy Monroe. *Big Game Hunting*. New York, NY: Rosen Central, 2011.

Sapp, Rick. *Trophy Bowhunting: Plan the Hunt of a Lifetime, then Bag One for the Record Books*. Mechanicsburg, PA: Stackpole Books, 2006.

Underwood, Lamar, ed. *The Greatest Hunting Stories Ever Told*. New York, NY: Lyons Press, 2004.

Wolny, Philip. *Avoiding Danger on the Hunt*. New York, NY: Rosen Central, 2013.

Young, G.O. *Alaskan Yukon Trophies Won and Lost*. Prescott, AZ: Wolfe Publishing Company, 2009.

Bibliography

Arizona Antelope Foundation. "B&C World Record 2000 Dylan Woods." Retrieved March 2012 (http://www.azantelope.org/World_Record/Dylan_Woods/dylan_woods.html).

Balfourd, Keith. "Polar Bear." *Petersen's Hunting*. Retrieved March 2012 (http://archives.petersenshunting.com/content/polar-bear).

Beatty, Mike. "Ohio's Amazing Beatty Buck." NorthAmericanWhitetail.com, September 22, 2010. Retrieved February 2012 (http://www.northamericanwhitetail.com/2010/09/22/trophybucks_naw_aa901beatty).

Boone and Crockett Club. "B&C's World Records." Retrieved February 2012 (http://www.boone-crockett.org/bgRecords/WorldRecords.asp?area=bgRecords).

Boone and Crockett Club. "Field Judging North American Big Game." Retrieved February 2012 (http://www.boone-crockett.org/bgRecords/records_FieldJudging_main.asp?area=bgRecords&ID=05EC63E2&se=1).

Broder, Craig. "Broder Buck: World Record Non-typical." *King's Outdoor World*, Fall 2012. Retrieved February 2012 (http://club.kingsoutdoorworld.com/magazine/fall2002/broder_buck.shtml).

Burkhead, Lynn. "Arizona Archer Franklin Arrows Potential World-Record, Non-Typical Bull." ESPNOutdoors.com, March 7, 2004. Retrieved March 2012 (http://tucsonhunting.com/News_Detail.php?g=news1100000200).

Burkhead, Lynn. "Ex-NFL Player Tackles World-Record Wapiti." ESPNOutdoors.com, January 12, 2006. Retrieved March 2012 (http://www.rmarchery.com/_hunting+news.html).

Cintorino, Pete. "Camp Quagmire: For This Veteran Bowhunter, a World Caribou Transforms Tribulation to Jubilation." *Bowhunter*, August 1, 2006. Retrieved March 2012 (http://www.thefreelibrary.com/amp+Quagmire%3A+for+this+veteran+bowhunter,+a+world+caribou+transforms...-a0147466628).

Creative Publishing editors. *Dressing & Cooking Wild Game: From Field to Table: Big Game, Small Game, Upland Birds, and Waterfowl*. Minnetonka, MN: Creative Publishing International, 2000.

DelHomme, P. J. "The Top 40 Biggest Moose Ever Taken." OutdoorLife.com. Retrieved March 2012 (http://www.outdoorlife.com/photos/gallery/hunting/big-game/moose/2012/02/top-40-biggest-moose-ever-taken?photo=1).

The Free Library. "Still Standing: George Shurtleff's Record Still Stands, and He's Still Bowhunting Blacktails." Retrieved February 2012 (http://www.thefreelibrary.com/still+standing%3A+George+Shurtleff%27s+record+still+stands,+and+he%27s...-a0166481539).

Gibson, Dan. "The Columbian Blacktail Deer." BlacktailCountry.com. Retrieved February 2012 (http://www.blacktailcountry.com/html/blkpage.htm).

Hunt Fair Chase. "Hunting Ethics." Retrieved March 2012 (http://www.huntfairchase.com/index.php/fuseaction/ethics.now).

Jones, J.Y. *One Man, One Rifle, One Land: Hunting All Species of Big Game in North America*. Huntington Beach, CA: Safari Press, 2001.

KingsOutdoorWorld.com. "World Record Typical Mule Deer—Burris Buck." Retrieved March 2012 (http://club.kingsoutdoorworld.com/gallery/2003/gallery_md1003.shtml).

Landers, Rich. "World-Record Goat Certified." *Spokesman-Review*, May 13, 2007. Retrieved February 2012 (http://www.spokesman.com/stories/2007/may/13/world-record-goat-certified).

Mandile, Tony. "World Record Coues Buck!" *Game and Fish*, October 4, 2010. Retrieved February 2012 (http://www.gameandfishmag.com/2010/10/04/hunting_whitetail-deer-hunting_rm_aa084603a/).

McKean, Andrew. "New World Record Elk?" *Outdoor Life*. Retrieved March 1, 2012 (http://www.outdoorlife.com/articles/hunting/2008/10/new-world-record-elk#. Retrieved March 1, 2012).

Miller, Lester. "Boone and Crockett's World Record Columbia Blacktail Deer." *Blacktail Legends of the Pacific Northwest*. Retrieved February 2012 (http://www.nwbiggame.com).

Nickens, T. Edward. *The Total Outdoorsman Manual*. San Francisco, CA: Weldon Owen, 2011.

Patrick, Tom. "Local Hunter Gets World Record Two Decades After Kill." *Yukon News*, September 10, 2010. Retrieved March 2012 (http://www.yukon-news.com/sports/19580).

Perich, Shawn, and Michael Furman. *Whitetail Hunting: Top-Notch Strategies for Hunting North America's Most Popular Big-Game Animal*. Chanhassen, MN: Creative Publishing International, 2004.

Pope and Young Club. "World Records by Species." Retrieved March 2012 (http://www.pope-young.org/world-records_main.asp).

Stephens, Flint. "Hunting Preparations That Help Insure Post-Kill Success." BigGameHunt.net, September 15, 2011. Retrieved March 2012 (http://www.biggamehunt.net/articles/hunting-preparations-help-insure-post-kill-success).

Sutton, Keith. "Record Quest: Pronghorn Antelope." *Outdoor Life*. Retrieved March 2012 (http://www.outdoorlife.com/node/45146).

Triplett, Todd. *Big-Game Taxidermy: A Complete Guide to Deer, Antelope, and Elk*. Guilford, CT: Lyons Press, 2006.

Wegner, Rob. "Johnson Buck Still King After 44 Years." *Deer and Deer Hunting*. Retrieved March 2012 (http://www.deeranddeerhunting.com/buck-shots/johnson-buck-still-king-after-44-years).

Whelen, Townsend. *Big Game Hunting*. Whitefish, MT: Kessinger Publishing, LLC, 2008.

The Wildlife Society. "The North American Model of Wildlife Conservation and Public Trust Doctrine." Retrieved April 2012 (http://joomla.wildlife.org/index.php?id=171&option=com_content&task=view).

Zieser, Marvin. "Antelope Hunt 1995: World Record Story." *Trophy Hunter*, Winter 1996. Retrieved April 2012 (http://www.azantelope.org/World_Record/Marvin_Zieser/Marvin_Zieser.pdf).

INDEX

About the Author

Christine Poolos is a writer and editor who lives in New York City. A native of rural Pennsylvania, she remembers the excitement of deer hunting season and watching hunters return to town with trophies tied to their trucks.

About the Consultant

Benjamin Cowan has more than twenty years of both big game and small game hunting experience. In addition to being an avid hunter, Cowan is also a member of many conservation organizations. He currently resides in west Tennessee.

Photo Credits

Cover, back cover (background), pp. 1, 3, 6, 9, 11, 18, 20, 28, 32, 34, 41, 45, 47, 49 © iStockphoto.com/Ryan Lane; pp. 5, 17 iStockphoto/Thinkstock; p. 7 Matt Carr/Workbook Stock/Getty Images; pp. 8, 10, 12, 21, 42, 44 © AP Images; p. 14 Bruce MacQueen/Shutterstock.com; p. 19 Jeff Banke/Shutterstock.com; p. 22 Visuals Unlimited, Inc./Patrick Endres/Getty Images; p. 23 Philippe Henry/Oxford Scientific/Getty Images; p. 25 Earl Harper/Aurora/Getty Images; p. 29 John E Marriott/All Canada Photos/Getty Images; p. 33 Photo by Daryl L. Hunter – The Hole Picture/Flickr/Getty Images; p. 35 Tom Brakefield/Stockbyte/Thinkstock; p. 38 Carl Iwasaki/Time & Life Pictures/Getty Images; p. 39 neelsky/Shutterstock.com; p. 43 John Warburton-Lee/AWL Images/Getty Images; p. 46 Danita Delimont/Gallo Images/Getty Images; p. 48 Wichita Eagle/McClatchy-Tribune/Getty Images; p. 50 Judy Kennamer/Shutterstock.com; p. 51 Nate A./Shutterstock.com; p. 52 Sibylle Fendt/Getty Images; cover and interior (camouflage patterns) © iStockphoto.com/molotovcoketail; back cover and interior (figure silhouettes) Hemera/Thinkstock; back cover (grass silhouette) iStockphoto.com/Makhnach_M; interior (figure silhouette) © iStockphoto.com/Michael Olson.

Designer: Nicole Russo; Photo Researcher: Karen Huang